POETRY STARS

A Treasury Of Verse

Edited By Donna Samworth

First published in Great Britain in 2023 by:

YoungWriters®
Est. 1991

Young Writers
Remus House
Coltsfoot Drive
Peterborough
PE2 9BF
Telephone: 01733 890066
Website: www.youngwriters.co.uk

Printed and bound in the UK by BookPrintingUK
Website: www.bookprintinguk.com
YB0527D

FOREWORD

Welcome to a fun-filled book of poems!

Here at Young Writers, we are delighted to introduce our new poetry competition for KS1 pupils, Poetry Stars. Pupils could choose to write an acrostic, sense poem or riddle to introduce them to the world of poetry. Giving them this framework allowed the young writers to open their imaginations to a range of topics of their choice, and encouraged them to include other literary techniques such as similes and description.

From family and friends, to animals and places, these pupils have shaped and crafted their ideas brilliantly, showcasing their budding creativity in verse.

We live and breathe creativity here at Young Writers – it gives us life! We want to pass our love of the written word onto the next generation and what better way to do that than to celebrate their writing by publishing it in a book!

Each awesome little poet in this book should be super proud of themselves, and now they've got proof of their imagination and their ideas when they first started creative writing to look back on in years to come! We hope you will delight in these poems as much as we have.

CONTENTS

Rowan Sall (6)	59
Fallon Boyle (7)	60
Bethany Payne (6)	61
Evelyn Coward (6)	62
Erin Courtneidge (6)	63
Charlie Anderson (7)	64
Leo Al-Tahan (5)	65
Charlie O'Connell (7)	66
Ryan Smith (6)	67
Harry Anderson (7)	68
Charlie McFarlane (5)	69
Ava Hebbert (5)	70

Sacred Heart RC Primary School, Battersea

Kenaya Nlendi (8)	71
Louisse-Margarette Nepomuceno (8)	72
Aaliyah Fulong (8)	73
Gael Boa (8)	74
Emily Hayler (9)	75
Ivor Somorjay (8)	76
Saskia Allen (9)	77
Amelia Stuart (8)	78
Artemis Christou (8)	79
Sophia Saggar (8)	80
Panos Christou (8)	81
Martina Barbarossa (8)	82
Lucianna Okoli (8)	83
Dylan Mora Cardona (9)	84
Malakai Ramirez (9)	85
Aaron Etse (8)	86
Jael Johnson (8)	87
Isobel Capps (8)	88
Konrad Sokol (8)	89
Jacob Orenzo-Easton (8)	90
Marcus Rodney (8)	91
Isaiah Parris (8)	92

St Andrews CE (A) Primary School, North Kilworth

Siara Cooke (8)	93
Logan Fairgrieve-Sealey (6)	94
Maisie Shuff (6)	95
Kingsley Partridge (7)	96
Benjamin Mukombo (8)	97
Katherine Sperry (6)	98
Alba-Rose Frake (8)	99
Tyler Oswin (8)	100
Boston Sharpe (6)	101
William Harding (6)	102
Douglas Higgins (7)	103

St John The Baptist RC Primary School, Fauldhouse

Elyse Zegveldt (10)	104
Millie (10)	106
Max M (11)	108
Lilyrose (10)	110
Brooke Howley (11)	112
Kaiden Gardiner (11)	114
Conlan Smith (11)	116
Lena Wawrzak	118
Alina Fluture (10)	119
Cian O'Driscoll (11)	120
Sienna (11)	121
Kyla Wilson (9)	122
Macie Holt (8)	123
Oliviajo Robb (9)	124
Charlie Green (8)	125
Gary Webster (11)	126
Keir Brown (8)	127
Mia Coleman (9)	128
Marcel Wawrzak (9)	129
Campbell Young (9)	130
Kayla Paterson (6) & Declan	131
Rhegan O'Driscoll (6)	132
Leon Gillespie (5)	133
Lewis Macleod (6)	134
Maisie Delaney (6)	135
Safiyyah Sowe (6)	136

St Mary's Catholic Primary School, Fleetwood

Hristiana Atlanasova (9)	137
Lily Martin (9)	138
Kobey Reece (10)	140
Molly Milhench (9)	142
Karolyn Hristova (11)	144
Florence Martinez (10)	146
Ralica Parapanova (10)	148
Ruby-Lea Mynott Ward (9)	149
Callum Watson (10)	150
Jessica Grimshaw (10)	151
Lucy Rose (10)	152
Layla Carney (10)	153
Gracie Penton (10)	154
Mateusz Krysztofinska (11)	155
Daisey Gawne (10)	156
Georgi Mitov (10)	157
Blake Slinger (9)	158
Conner Watson (10)	159
Elliot Wilson (10)	160

Stanley St Andrew's CE Primary School, Stanley

Finley Marshall (7)	161

Starcross Primary School, Starcross

George Kebell (11)	162

Strandtown Primary School, Belfast

Violet Wilson (7)	163
Shaun Mathew (8)	164
Lucie Wilson (7)	165
Yuriy Hramov (7)	166
Matthew Lucas (7)	167
Saul Farrell (8)	168

Windsor Park CE Middle School, Uttoxeter

Sian Keeling (9)	169
Holly Chapman (10)	170
Thea Clarke (9)	172
Nancy Newton (9)	173
Joseph Clarke (9)	174
Connor Wilkes (9)	175
Ellie-May Wilson (9)	176
William Chandler (9)	177
Lewis Frost (9)	178
Maisie Rowntree (9)	179
Henry Coates (10)	180
Corey Lampitt (9)	181
Benjamin Haywood (9)	182
Emilia Skinner (9)	183

THE POEMS

Autumn

A utumn leaves come down everywhere
U nder the layers of leaves, damp grass
covers me
T ight branches cover the floor
U nique leaves cover me like a cosy blanket
M isty fog lies everywhere
N ew dark clouds pour with rain.

Poppy Payton (8)
Bracken Leas Primary School, Brackley

Blossom

B eing themselves under the sun
L ight and bright baby plants
O h my favourites
S pring beauties in the fields
S uper smell
O dd one out
M arvellous flowers.

Florrie Willmore (8)

Bracken Leas Primary School, Brackley

Autumn

A kennings poem

Starry sky wisher
Bonfire lighter
Extra heater
Leaf rustler
Pumpkin carver
Conker picker
Pinecone finder
Sock wearer
Marshmallow toaster
Blanket snuggler
Soup slurper
Movie watcher
Chocolate lover.

Honey Bowman (8)
Bracken Leas Primary School, Brackley

Gymnastics

G ymnastics is the best
Y oung kids go there
M e and you can learn to jump
N iya is my favourite teacher
A t gymnastics it is fun
S plits are amazing
T umble tracks are cool
I t is tiring
C artwheels are the best
S traddle jumps are awesome.

Gracie Newcombe (6)
Fairfield Primary School, South Wigston

Football

F ootball is the best
O i, no bad tackles
O i, yellow card
T he player scores a goal
B lue boots I love
A ll of the players are cool
L ove it
L iverpool is my team!

Daniel Diaconu (6)
Fairfield Primary School, South Wigston

Dodgeball

D odgeball is fun

O ver the net

D odge the ball

G et them out

E veryone paying

B all in hand

A ttack the ball

L aunch it hard

L aunch it far!

Louie Simons (6)

Fairfield Primary School, South Wigston

Football

F ootball is good to play

O pen goal

O ver the net

T he goal is open

B ack of the net

A brilliant team

L eicester is my team

L eicester to win!

Romeo Chauhan (6)
Fairfield Primary School, South Wigston

Potatoes

P eel them

O ven cook your jackets

T ime to mash

A dd butter, yummy

T asty roasties

O n the hob chips

E xtra cheesy chips

S uper potato!

Joshua Wagstaff (6)

Fairfield Primary School, South Wigston

Lorelei

L orelei is playing horses

O range juice to drink, yum

R eally beautiful

E xcellent sister

L ove teddies

E njoys YouTube

I have lots of friends.

Lorelei Sawyers Short (6)

Fairfield Primary School, South Wigston

Football

F ootball every day

O i, no bad tackling!

O i, yellow card

T he goalie kicks

B eautiful ball

A ll the time

L ove it

L ap to warm up.

Zachary Spencer (6)

Fairfield Primary School, South Wigston

Hot Dog

H ave them on the BBQ

O nions not on mine

T omato ketchup

D elicious

O nions not on mine

G ot to eat it all up

S ausages are yummy.

Tallulah Brenson-Wright (6)

Fairfield Primary School, South Wigston

Marisa

M y friends are Elsie and Aairah
A nd I have another friend, Lucy
R ainbows are lovely
I love ice cream
S ports are fun
A nd I am six and crafty.

Marisa Patel (6)
Fairfield Primary School, South Wigston

Emelia

E xcellent at riding my bike

M y hair is brown

E yes are hazel

L ove playing football

I like to ride my scooter

A lways play with my friends.

Emelia Moore (6)

Fairfield Primary School, South Wigston

Aairah

A m a big fan of unicorns
A mazed by unicorns
I ce cream is the best
R ainbows are lovely
A m a good friend
H ot chocolate is yummy.

Aairah Mansoor (6)
Fairfield Primary School, South Wigston

Rayyan

R ayyan is obsessed with YouTube
A mazing person
Y ummy spaghetti
Y ummy yellow Skittles
A lways a fun boy
N ot a bad boy.

Rayyan Hammed (6)
Fairfield Primary School, South Wigston

Elsie

E than is my brother
L ilies are my favourite flower
S chool is fun
I go to Fairfield Primary School
E mily is my best friend.

Elsie Carter (7)

Fairfield Primary School, South Wigston

My Dog

M y dog is Milo
Y ou are lovely Milo

D o a twirl, Milo, good!
O utside Milo brings me balls
G ood dog, I love you!

Keira Broughton (6)

Fairfield Primary School, South Wigston

Ocean

O ctopuses live in the ocean
C oral is where fish sometimes live
E very day is excellent
A nimals live there
N ot empty.

William Bradbury (6)

Fairfield Primary School, South Wigston

Artist

A rt is beautiful

R eally colourful

T ie-dye tops

I nk or chalk?

S pectacular colours

T ry your best.

Jacob Keene (6)
Fairfield Primary School, South Wigston

Ocean

O ctopuses have tentacles
C rabs walk sideways
E very fish can swim
A lligators bite
N ever dry.

Jacob Rudkin (6)
Fairfield Primary School, South Wigston

Emily

E mily is a good girl

M y mum is creative

I am sweet

L ove you

Y ou are my friend.

Emily Hobbs (6)

Fairfield Primary School, South Wigston

Lucy

L ike to sing and dance

U nderwater swimming

C ute and adorable

Y ellow and blonde hair.

Lucy Basten (6)
Fairfield Primary School, South Wigston

Vet

V et looks after pets

E xcellent at helping

T akes care of animals.

Tilly-Rae Mayes Henfrey (6)
Fairfield Primary School, South Wigston

Art

A rtistic painting

R uby-red painting

T otally awesome pictures.

Sarahi Hundal (6)

Fairfield Primary School, South Wigston

Halloween

It tastes like iced doughnuts on a string,
cold apples in cold water and juicy and
delicious sweets
It smells like my shiny sweet burning
pumpkin and strong-scented candles
It sounds like high-pitched howling wolves
and squelching footsteps from rattling
bones of skeletons
It looks like ghosts gliding through the
haunted house and black bats gliding over
the moon
It feels like freezing water and sticky toffee
apples sticking my teeth together.

Robin French (7)

Grange Primary School, Dundee

Halloween

It tastes like cold wet apples and yummy tasty eyeball Haribos going down your throat
It sounds like rattling gravestones, crackling thunder and spooky ghosts scaring me
It smells like creepy witches, cauldrons and pumpkins rotting
It looks like gigantic spiders, floating ghosts and evil pumpkins, flying bats and haunted houses
It feels like hard wooden doors, warm spiderwebs, hairy pumpkins and sticky toffee apples.

Cole Easton (8)

Grange Primary School, Dundee

Halloween

It tastes like chewy marshmallow eyeballs
with chocolate sauce
It sounds like skeletons squelching in the
mud with rumbling thunder behind
It smells like smoky candles melting in the
sun and rotten gooey pumpkins
It looks like scary ghosts flying in the air and
black hairy spiders crawling around your
house
It feels like giant smooth pumpkins and
hairy spiderwebs.

Harvey Henehan (7)

Grange Primary School, Dundee

Halloween

It tastes like sweet toffee apples and
chocolate eyeballs
It sounds like creaking floorboards and
werewolves howling
It smells like sweet-scented candles burning
in my terrifying pumpkin
It looks like bubbling cauldrons with creepy
black cats, jack-o'-lanterns and a haunted
house
It feels like misty cauldrons with tangly
cobwebs and a smooth giant pumpkin.

Alisha Alif (7)

Grange Primary School, Dundee

Halloween

It tastes like chewy sticky eyes and hot
marshmallow hot chocolate
It sounds like zombies groaning and
screaming in terror
It smells like fear, damp leaves and pumpkin
pie
It looks like a bubbling cauldron, a giant
spooky spider and a big black cat
It feels like fluffy warm spiderwebs, a sticky
toffee apple and slimy spooky pumpkins.

Rosie Matthews (7)
Grange Primary School, Dundee

Halloween

It tastes like squishy gummies kids have
been scared with by parents
It sounds like shaking gravestones moving
around the squelchy mud
It smells like smoky candles when people
have gone out in terrifying costumes
It looks like a nasty tarantula biting people's
long arms
It feels like fluffy cat fur lying on the side of
the road.

Florence McQueen (8)
Grange Primary School, Dundee

Halloween

It tastes like gooey chewy little sweets that get stuck in my teeth
It sounds like werewolves howling through the night when the moon is shining
It smells like damp leaves that have fallen off a tree
It looks like a big scary haunted house in the middle of nowhere
It feels like wet big seeds that have come out of my scary pumpkin.

Ethan Caldwell (8)
Grange Primary School, Dundee

Halloween

It tastes like toffee apples and hot chocolate with squirty cream and marshmallows.
It sounds like cackling witches and hooting owls.
It smells like damp leaves and woodfires.
It looks like scary, spooky skeletons shaking their bones and carved pumpkins.
It makes me feel happy, excited, scared and awesome.

Olivia Hutcheon (8)

Grange Primary School, Dundee

Halloween

It tastes like sweet toffee apples on a scary
Halloween night
It sounds like scary skeletons squelching in
the mud
It smells like scary witches burning wood on
a fireplace
It looks like scary cauldrons cooking the
witch's tea, it is very hot
It feels like not nice fluffy warm cobwebs.

Hollie Raitt (8)
Grange Primary School, Dundee

Halloween

It tastes like sweet toffee apples melting in
my mouth
It sounds like scary creaking doors at
midnight in the dark
It smells like smoky strawberry candles and
creamy pumpkin soup
It looks like a big orange and black spider
with pink and blue eyes
It feels like wet warm cobwebs.

Gracie Whyte (7)
Grange Primary School, Dundee

Halloween

It tastes like sweet, sticky toffee apples
melting in my throat
It sounds like cackling witches and their
bubbling potions
It smells like sweet, creamy pumpkin pie
It looks like scary black cats staring at me
It feels like freezing cold water on my face
when I bob for apples.

Sophie McGlashan (8)
Grange Primary School, Dundee

Halloween

It tastes like chewy, big, juicy red
marshmallow cake
It sounds like a huge crack of thunder
It smells like burning flaming orange and
red wood
It looks like dead creepy skeletons lying on
the black basement floor
It feels like big warm sticky goo and black
spiderwebs.

Max Kelly (8)
Grange Primary School, Dundee

Halloween

It tastes like juicy apples for dunking
It sounds like moaning zombies, bubbling
cauldrons and howling wolves
It smells like rotten pumpkins and smoky
fire
It looks like scary costumes shiny from the
shop
It feels like hard apples in the water and
misty cauldrons.

Sophie Wilson (7)
Grange Primary School, Dundee

Halloween

It tastes like sweet toffee apple tricking down my throat
It sounds like pumpkins laughing and howling
It smells like rotten pumpkins and sticky toffee apples
It looks like a spooky haunted house with wolves in it
It feels like fluffy spiderwebs and fluffy cats.

Megan McGovern (8)

Grange Primary School, Dundee

Halloween

It tastes like juicy pumpkin pie and tasty
soft cream
It sounds like zombies squelching in the
mud
It smells like smelly, soaking-wet dogs
It looks like dead, spooky skeletons in a
spooky house
It feels like fluffy warm spiderwebs.

Savannah Fraser (8)

Grange Primary School, Dundee

Halloween

It tastes like crunchy eyeballs
It sounds like creaking, scared, screeching
zombies
It looks like haunted houses with skeletons
cracking their bones
It smells like the damp smoky candles
It feels like sticky toffee with icing.

Charlotte Proctor (7)

Grange Primary School, Dundee

Halloween

It tastes like tasty caramel apples
It sounds like noisy zombies going out into
the street
It smells like hot chocolate with roasted
marshmallows
It looks like scary hanging spider
decorations
It feels like fluffy spiderwebs.

Lucas Madden (8)

Grange Primary School, Dundee

Halloween

It tastes like burning hot chocolate and
scrumptious pie
It sounds like howling loud wolves from the
top of a mountain
It smells like a burning hot, smoky fire
It looks like a black cat grinning
It feels like a fluffy cat.

Iona Black (7)

Grange Primary School, Dundee

Halloween

It tastes like creamy chocolate sweets
It sounds like creaking floorboards
It smells like creamy pumpkin pie
It looks like a creepy haunted house
It feels like spiderwebs on my face.

Mila Willaims (7)

Grange Primary School, Dundee

Halloween

It tastes like eyeball cupcakes
It sounds like a giant spooky spider
It smells like scented smoky candles
It looks like a full orange moon
It feels like a spooky black cat.

Amelia Skelly (8)
Grange Primary School, Dundee

Fun At The Playground

P eople having fun

L aughing on the roundabout

A dults are sitting on the bench

Y ippeee, I am going on the slide

G oing on the climbing frame

R iding on the rocking horse

O utside is nice and fresh

U nder the tunnel

N early time to go home

D ear Mummy, thank you for taking me.

Amelia Khan (7)

Oaklands Primary School, Welwyn

My Pet Giraffe

G ary is my pet giraffe

I n the evening he has a bath

R unning really fast and far

A nd to keep up we go by car

F ood and drink are his favourite things

F ather always takes out the bins

E vening is the best time as I spend it with my pet giraffe.

Molly Campbell (6)

Oaklands Primary School, Welwyn

Animals

Dogs are playful and loving
Koalas are fuzzy and like to sleep all day
Pandas are fascinating animals and they
love eating bamboo
Tiger cubs are my favourite animals as they
do not have to have showers
This is because their mum licks their coat.

Tenzin Pema (6)
Oaklands Primary School, Welwyn

We All Love Sweets

S weets are yummy, sweets are tasty
W hen I eat sweets I feel happy
E xciting flavours, sour and fizzy
E ating sweets keeps me busy
T angy, tingling, satisfying on my tongue
S ucking sweets all day long!

Harrison Smith (6)

Oaklands Primary School, Welwyn

Super Cheetah

C heetah runs faster

H as very sharp teeth

E veryone is scared of him

E ats and munches on meat

T iger is not a cheetah's friend

A mazing, smart and sharp

H e is a handsome cheetah.

Keshav Attarwala (6)

Oaklands Primary School, Welwyn

The Scary Dragon!

D own in the dark cave

R unning away from the beast

A big fierce monster appears at the door

G roaning and growing in the mist

O ur spots and teeth are shining in the moon

N ow I breathe fire.

Dexter Hatt (6)

Oaklands Primary School, Welwyn

Hamster

H amsters feel safe in tubes
A lways scurrying about
M ake great pets
S tore food in their cheeks
T hey are soft to stroke
E veryone loves to pet them
R eally lively at night.

Abigail Hassan (6)
Oaklands Primary School, Welwyn

My Favourite Animal

S wim from side to side
H undreds of different sharks in the sea
A great white is the most dangerous
R eef sharks can swim close to the surface
K iller nets kill many fish and sharks.

Lou De Decker (6)

Oaklands Primary School, Welwyn

Birthday Fun

B alloons pop

I love presents

R eally yummy cake

T ime for a party

H appy birthday

D ay of fun

A year older

Y es, it's my birthday!

Mila Whinnett (6)

Oaklands Primary School, Welwyn

Garden

G rass is everywhere

A pples grow on trees

R ed is the colour of roses

D igging up vegetables is so much fun

E veryone plays in the sun

N ature is all around.

Daniella Cole (7)

Oaklands Primary School, Welwyn

Charlie's Banana Poem

B rown they can go
A nd they are hard to find in the snow
N ice snacks they can be
A nd yellow you can see
N ight monkeys like them too
A nd toodle-oo!

Charlie Mitchell (6)

Oaklands Primary School, Welwyn

I Love Dancing

D o you like my dancing?
A ll the children are on the dancefloor
N ow I can jump and wiggle
C ircles spinning to the loud music
E veryone loves to dance.

Aurora Herbert (6)

Oaklands Primary School, Welwyn

Exploring The Woods Team

W e climb trees up high
O wls go tu-whit tu-whoo in the night
O ver the big hill we run
D own by the stream we find tadpoles
S quirrels bury acorns.

Florence Hatt (6)

Oaklands Primary School, Welwyn

Sunny Beach Day

B usy days by the sea
E veryone loves splashing in the sea
A nd playing in the sand
C razy golf is crazy fun
H ot days, let's go in the chalet.

Charlotte Roberts (6)

Oaklands Primary School, Welwyn

Giraffes

G iraffes are tall
I like them all
R unning when they
A re scared
F rom Africa
F ood is leaves from a tree
E xtremely calm.

Rowan Sall (6)

Oaklands Primary School, Welwyn

Pippin

P erfect dog

I walk Pippin in the woods

P lease be kind to my dog

P lease, my doggy has dog cookies

I can jump high

N ice dog.

Fallon Boyle (7)

Oaklands Primary School, Welwyn

Winter

W rap up warm

I t is cold

N ight-time for some animals

T rees are dull

E xcited for Christmas

R eady for snow.

Bethany Payne (6)

Oaklands Primary School, Welwyn

I Love Barbie

B eautiful blue eyes

A nice smile

R uby-red

B londe and shiny hair

I love to play with her

E verywhere.

Evelyn Coward (6)

Oaklands Primary School, Welwyn

Zadie

Z ebra is her best toy

A rt is what she likes to do

D addy plays with her

I nterested in toys

E rin is her cousin.

Erin Courtneidge (6)

Oaklands Primary School, Welwyn

Silly Ninja Charlie

K arate kicks

A mazing moves

R eally good fun

A t any ability

T actical kicks

E nergise your body.

Charlie Anderson (7)

Oaklands Primary School, Welwyn

Lego

L egoland is lots of fun.

E very ride is awesome.

G oing there makes me happy.

O h, my favourite is the Sky Lion!

Leo Al-Tahan (5)

Oaklands Primary School, Welwyn

Lego

L ego is fun to build

E veryone can join in

G old pieces are my favourite

O range bricks are bright.

Charlie O'Connell (7)

Oaklands Primary School, Welwyn

Howling Wolf

W et nose

O n their own

L ive in a pack

F ierce with fur and related to foxes.

Ryan Smith (6)

Oaklands Primary School, Welwyn

Man On The Moon

M an on the moon
O h so far away
O ne rocket far away
N eil says goodbye.

Harry Anderson (7)
Oaklands Primary School, Welwyn

Lego

L ego is a toy

E veryone can play

G irls and boys

O pen the pack.

Charlie McFarlane (5)

Oaklands Primary School, Welwyn

The Naughty Dog

L udo

U nder a cow

D ad says no

O h no, Ludo bit the cow.

Ava Hebbert (5)

Oaklands Primary School, Welwyn

About The Stars And Solar System

S tars and bars, stars are Abraham's children

O n the grass you lie down and see the stars at night

L ittle bars and little stars, little stars can be seen in every country

A ll bars don't have stars, they should build a new star bar

R unning a bar is hard but running stars isn't

S eeing stars and bars, also jars! What else?

Y ou see colourful jars with stars

S tars near Mars

T he jar is far, let me reach it

E at a star dessert on Mars

M e, I love stars.

Kenaya Nlendi (8)

Sacred Heart RC Primary School, Battersea

Louisse

L ooking forward to writing something for you

O bserving the silence that's what I will do

U nderstanding what you like is what I'm into

I nteresting thoughts, that's what I'm up to

S earching for an answer, that's the clue

S omething special just awaits you

E xpectations will be high but anything just for you.

Louisse-Margarette Nepomuceno (8)
Sacred Heart RC Primary School, Battersea

Monkeys

M y favourite animal is a monkey

O oooh-oooh-ahhhh-ahhhh it says when it is angry or hungry

N aughty, funny, playful and cheeky

K ind of like me!

E ating yummy bananas makes them healthy, strong and happy

Y ou can always see them climbing and swinging up the trees

S illy but curious and smart, that is how they are known to be.

Aaliyah Fulong (8)

Sacred Heart RC Primary School, Battersea

Playground

P layground is fun

L ay down under the sun

A treat for the children and me

Y es, let's play with Sandy

G reat ziplines to ride on

R eady, steady, go!

O range juice for you and me

U mbrella to cover the sun

N ow let's have some more fun

D id you say goodbye?

Gael Boa (8)

Sacred Heart RC Primary School, Battersea

Family

F ull of lots of loving and happy memories

A mazing and fun days out together

M ummy, Daddy, Chloe, Mollie and John are my family

I love them all so much

L ove to chill, watch a movie and eat popcorn together

Y es, having big family cuddles is the best and I feel very lucky to have a family like mine.

Emily Hayler (9)

Sacred Heart RC Primary School, Battersea

Puddings

P erfectly baked spongey cake
U nique, fruity, crunchy crumble
D elicious yoghurt slides down my throat
D igging into my gingerbread biscuits
I instruct you to buy these fruits
N othing beats pudding
G listening ice cream scoops in the bowl
S atisfied, my dish is done.

Ivor Somorjay (8)

Sacred Heart RC Primary School, Battersea

Holiday

H ot and lovely weather

O live trees around

L oveable, peaceful and very calm sea

I am relaxing and having a cup of tea

D elicious tasty food on top

A ll day at the beach, very hot

Y awning, lying, swinging and trying to relax.

Saskia Allen (9)

Sacred Heart RC Primary School, Battersea

Excited

E mily loves pictures

X ylophones are colourful

C reative paintings are from creative people

I t's a wonderful life

T igers in the wild

E lectric lights flashing

D ancing to fast music.

Amelia Stuart (8)

Sacred Heart RC Primary School, Battersea

Amazing Artemis

A mazing me, you'll see

R unning up and down with my friends

T ime is up, ten out of ten!

E legantly dancing like a swan

M agnificently doing my things

I 'm definitely

S uper!

Artemis Christou (8)

Sacred Heart RC Primary School, Battersea

Sophia Saggar

S uper
O rdinary
P retty
H yper
 I ndependent
A mazing

S illy
A ctress
G ood
G orgeous
A ctress
R oyal.

Sophia Saggar (8)
Sacred Heart RC Primary School, Battersea

Greece, Old Greece

G reat time in Greece

R eal fun there

E xcellent beaches and hospitality

E verything you eat is delicious

C old you say? Hot I say!

E la tóra = come now!

Panos Christou (8)

Sacred Heart RC Primary School, Battersea

The Month October

C old

O ctober

A lways makes people

T ired

D ozy

A ll

Y ear

H old

A ll the warmth

T ight.

Martina Barbarossa (8)

Sacred Heart RC Primary School, Battersea

Kitty

K itty is my black and white cat
I love you so much
T he cutest cat in the world
T ootsies like little baked beans
Y ou're my best friend kitty.

Lucianna Okoli (8)
Sacred Heart RC Primary School, Battersea

Dylan

D ay by day going to school
Y ou will see him on the basketball court
L oving and kind
A t school with his friends
N ever forgets to play the piano.

Dylan Mora Cardona (9)

Sacred Heart RC Primary School, Battersea

Family

F un and games

A lways there for me

M akes me happy

I love them

L aughing all the time

Y ou can always rely on family.

Malakai Ramirez (9)

Sacred Heart RC Primary School, Battersea

Tablet

T he player is you

A dd your weapons

B ad guys on the game

L et them fight

E at for energy

T ake your tablet today!

Aaron Etse (8)

Sacred Heart RC Primary School, Battersea

All About The Cinema

Cameras
Dark, noisy
Chatting, screaming, shouting
Popcorn, drinks, chocolate, ice cream
Watching, crying, laughing
Scared, upset
Screen.

Jael Johnson (8)
Sacred Heart RC Primary School, Battersea

Ice And Fire

Ice
Jagged, frozen
Freezing, melting, shivering
Snow, icicles, matches, flames
Burning, blazing, crackling
Fierce, ferocious
Fire.

Isobel Capps (8)

Sacred Heart RC Primary School, Battersea

Bike

B ell on the steering wheel

I am very good at riding my bike

K ilometres on the metre

E verybody riding their bike.

Konrad Sokol (8)

Sacred Heart RC Primary School, Battersea

Hot And Cold

Hot
Burning, boiling
Cold, frosty, freezing
Sunny, bright, melting, shining
Snowing, icy, shivering
Roasting, baking
Frosty.

Jacob Orenzo-Easton (8)
Sacred Heart RC Primary School, Battersea

Up And Down

Up
Top, high
Climbing, ascending, growing
Moon, sun, chandelier, clouds
Dropping, descending, falling
Dripping, below
Down.

Marcus Rodney (8)

Sacred Heart RC Primary School, Battersea

My Mum's Worst Nightmare

Stick insect
Brown, green
Crawling, jumping, moving
Leaf, roof, eats, long
Moves, eats, lots
Green, brown
Blend.

Isaiah Parris (8)

Sacred Heart RC Primary School, Battersea

At Harvest Time I Can See

I can see yummy fresh wheat
It smells of tasty bread
I can feel the wheat as soft as a fluffy hamster
I can hear a combine harvester chopping the wheat in the field
I can taste delicious juicy tomatoes as red as lava
You can also see a big gigantic tractor as blue as the sky
I can hear the factory making wheat into bread
I can taste pumpkin pie like candy with custard.

Siara Cooke (8)
St Andrews CE (A) Primary School, North Kilworth

Harvest

In the harvest season I can see tractors
going into the barn with lots of vegetables
all the way to the top of the trailer
I can smell sweetcorn cooking in the oven
I can feel spikes on the pumpkin stalk when
I carry the pumpkin
I can taste the juicy red tomatoes on my
tongue
I can hear the combine harvesters chopping
the corn.

Logan Fairgrieve-Sealey (6)
St Andrews CE (A) Primary School, North Kilworth

Harvest

At harvest time I can see big, round
pumpkins with long stalks in the field
Smells of tasty fruits and vegetables
I can feel the grains of wheat as small as
sand in my hands
Sounds of noisy farmers in their giant
tractors collecting the wheat
I can taste juicy tomatoes
Harvest is a great time of the year.

Maisie Shuff (6)

St Andrews CE (A) Primary School, North Kilworth

Harvest

At harvest time I can see the noisy combine harvesters
Smells of delicious pumpkin pie as sweet as candy
I can feel the heaviness of a pumpkin which is the size of a boulder
Sounds of birds sweeping down
I can taste apple crumble with sugary custard
Harvest is the best!

Kingsley Partridge (7)

St Andrews CE (A) Primary School, North Kilworth

Harvest

At harvest time I can see birds getting
scared by the scarecrows
Smells of pumpkin pie fill the air
I can feel fresh ripe juicy pumpkin on my
fingertips
Sounds of food getting plucked out of the
fine rich soil
I can taste juicy, ripe, plump pumpkins.

Benjamin Mukombo (8)

St Andrews CE (A) Primary School, North Kilworth

Harvest

I can see pumpkins on the ground
I can smell pumpkins
I can feel pumpkins as I roll the pumpkins
down the hill
Sounds of pumpkins cracking
I can taste pumpkins as they crunch in my
mouth
I get them stuck in my teeth.

Katherine Sperry (6)
St Andrews CE (A) Primary School, North Kilworth

At Harvest

I can see the big green combine harvester
Smells of fresh warm soft bread
I can feel the wheat waving in the wind
Sounds of wheat whistling in the winds
I can taste the delicious custard
I can taste pumpkin pie.

Alba-Rose Frake (8)

St Andrews CE (A) Primary School, North Kilworth

Harvest

At harvest time I can see big juicy pumpkins
I can smell porridge and pumpkins
I can touch mud in my hand
I can hear birds tweeting
I can taste sweetcorn and fresh juicy tomatoes
I can smell the tomatoes.

Tyler Oswin (8)
St Andrews CE (A) Primary School, North Kilworth

Harvest

At harvest time I can see pumpkins as big
as a boulder
I can feel and smell the pumpkin soup
I can feel the soft pumpkins
I can hear the sounds of the fire
I can taste pumpkin soup.

Boston Sharpe (6)

St Andrews CE (A) Primary School, North Kilworth

Harvest Time

At harvest time I can see naughty treats
Smell the pumpkins in the sheds
I can smell dirty potatoes
Sounds of the noisy harvest
I can taste pumpkin soup
I can smell candles.

William Harding (6)
St Andrews CE (A) Primary School, North Kilworth

Harvest

At harvest I can see delicious aubergines
ripened in the sun
I can smell pumpkin pie
I can feel slimy carrots as I rub them on my
skin
I can hear tractors rumbling.

Douglas Higgins (7)
St Andrews CE (A) Primary School, North Kilworth

My Traditional Poem

In the Amazon Rainforest rivers are strong
The rivers are long but it has to end at some
point
Some animals live on land and water
Animals are happy in their habitat
But it sadly has to end at some time

Around the world floods are happening
The water comes up but never stops
Our world is grey but it used to be as green
as grass
The clouds are black like inside a chimney
Half the world is dead my friend so that's
why we need to help

Sloths can't live in peace because of the
trees being down
You can't clean your mess up with a cloth,
it's not that easy
Animals are not okay because of all of this

Animals are dying with this big mess
There are more animals dying in the north

Wars are happening so we need to stop
planes soaring through the air and bombing
places
Some are sad or happy
Or some are scared or excited
People are in despair so please stop this
war before it's too late.

Elyse Zegveldt (10)

St John The Baptist RC Primary School, Fauldhouse

My Traditional Poem

Our world is dying, we have to make a change
Plastic is floating in the dark sea
Far in the forest, trees are falling down
Pandas and polar bears are at risk of dying
No one can save them unless we make a change

Our world is getting greyer every day
The animals are screaming for help but we're not listening
Our seas are turning plastic as far as we can see
What would we do if there was no life in the sea?

We can't let history replay itself again
Back then horrible things were done to animals
The world is ticking, come on, you have to get your head up now

So we can make a change before it's too late

I know we are trying our best to save the environment
But people are starting to get really judgemental
The wind is howling
We need to plant crops so that the world can breathe.

Millie (10)

St John The Baptist RC Primary School, Fauldhouse

My Traditional Poem

There is waste and rubbish in our sea
The sea is drying and dying
All of the animals are going to die and leave
And what are we doing to the sea?

The Amazon Rainforest is dying with ease
The animals are shouting
Please! Please! Please!
Give us some money, please!

Floods are coming
And the seas are rising
Places, houses, all in ruins
People and animals are also sad and
sighing.

Polar bears are crying
The penguins and seals are needing to
move

The Antarctic is slowly dying
The ice spikes are also drying

Trees, trees are getting cut down with ease
The oxygen is going to run out
The trees and animals are shouting
Please! Please! Please!
And we are just cutting them with ease.

Max M (11)
St John The Baptist RC Primary School, Fauldhouse

My Traditional Poem

Climate change and littering is killing the
animals all around the world
They are curled under the sea
The trees are getting killed more and more
every day
We are not letting them win ever again
It's getting out of hand
The animals are screeching for help
Covid-19 has affected everyone

Our sea is mostly plastic and the
environment is getting unhealthier every
day
Our world is getting greyer
It used to be as blue as the sky
The ice is melting so polar bears can't
breathe
They're screaming, "Help me!"

Killing animals for what?
What else can we do?

Lilyrose (10)
St John The Baptist RC Primary School, Fauldhouse

My Traditional Poem

Climate change is killing our environment
and these are the reasons why
Everything is dying off so keep everything
alive

People are littering, it's going into the sea
Killing these animals but what help are we?

Flash floods are coming, everyone is
panicking
The only way to help is by sending some of
our clothing

Wild forest fires are spreading more than
ever
Why isn't there a lever to turn off this
weather?

These are the reasons why our environment
is going extinct
Why are you still reading this?
Go and help sort this out!

Brooke Howley (11)

St John The Baptist RC Primary School, Fauldhouse

A Traditional Poem

The ocean is a mighty beast like the
Minotaur
It is as blue as the sky but as dark as night
It is as mean as a bull but as nice as a
bunny
So let's stop the pollution so the animals
don't die

The Earth might die so let us help it
We should stop all forest fires 'cause they
are bad
Let's help the animals not to lose their
home
Let's stop them from going extinct

The Amazon is all green
But some of the animals in it are becoming
extinct

So let's make sure they don't become
extinct
So they live longer.

Kaiden Gardiner (11)
St John The Baptist RC Primary School, Fauldhouse

My Traditional Poem

Putin's bombing Ukraine
Millions dying
People crying
It's a disaster
It's hard to go to the shop and get a bag of pasta

Plastic in the ocean
As far as the eye can see
Pollution is bad
We need to stop
If we don't the world will pop

Ice caps are melting
Water levels are rising
Polar bears are dying
They are all crying

Animals are becoming extinct
We will be extinct too

This is our world so please look after it
Before it's too late!

Conlan Smith (11)

St John The Baptist RC Primary School, Fauldhouse

A Traditional Poem

The environment is changing because of us
We have got to think quickly before time
runs out

If we keep littering our oceans there's going
to be lots of deaths caused by us

If we keep chopping down trees
No healthy air for us and lots of beautiful,
scary animals
There will be no homes for us

We have to take care of our beautiful
environment
Before trillions of animals will die

We have to take care of our environment
Before disasters come.

Lena Wawrzak
St John The Baptist RC Primary School, Fauldhouse

My Traditional Poem

People are littering, then they are tittering
They are now muttering
They don't know what they are doing
And the Earth is dying
Some places receive a disaster
Some people receive first-aid kits

Now they are sad
But then it is bad
The only one who can save us...
Is in the mirror
It is you
Don't be afraid
I'm not mad

Don't worry
'Cause next time we'll live happy again
On a new Earth
When it ends.

Alina Fluture (10)
St John The Baptist RC Primary School, Fauldhouse

A Traditional Poem

Roses are red, violets are blue
We will need to do things to help our planet
in 2022
We need to recycle our plastic, food and
paper
If we do this, we will find it better later

Earth Day, Earth Day comes once a year
But we should make our message clear
Clean the Earth each day
Make that a plan to stay

Earth Day, Earth Day comes once a year
Love and care for our Earth so dear.

Cian O'Driscoll (11)

St John The Baptist RC Primary School, Fauldhouse

My Traditional Poem

The ocean is as blue as the sky
Why are we letting it die?

The landfills are blowing away
Just let them breathe

The animals are screaming for help
Can't you hear their yelps?

We need to help these animals stay alive
Like the bees in the beehive.

Sienna (11)

St John The Baptist RC Primary School, Fauldhouse

Calm And Mad

Calm
Okay, joyful
Meditating, sitting, chilling
Friends, reading, talking over, not listening
Shouting, hitting, ignoring
Angry, cross
Mad.

Kyla Wilson (9)

St John The Baptist RC Primary School, Fauldhouse

Summer And Winter

Summer
Fun, boiling
Playing, swimming, running
Sunny, green, yummy, cold juice
Snowball fighting, building, drinking
Freezing, snow
Winter.

Macie Holt (8)

St John The Baptist RC Primary School, Fauldhouse

Land And Sea Animals

Land animals
Ground, dry
Walking, sitting, running
Fur, feet, flippers, gills
Swimming, bubbling, breathing
Soaking, wet
Sea animals.

Oliviajo Robb (9)

St John The Baptist RC Primary School, Fauldhouse

Summer And Winter

Summer
Fun, hot
Suntan, swimming, paddling
Suntan, holiday, snow, cold
Freezing, snowballing, building
Ice-cold, shivering
Winter.

Charlie Green (8)
St John The Baptist RC Primary School, Fauldhouse

My Traditional Poem

Gas and electricity prices have risen
We have to do something
Before people cry
We should do some recycling
And make the environment great!

Gary Webster (11)
St John The Baptist RC Primary School, Fauldhouse

Fire And Ice

Fire
Scorching, roasting
Burns, hurts, soars
Wood, lighter, water, freezer
Drink, dissolve, melting
Freezing, watery
Ice.

Keir Brown (8)
St John The Baptist RC Primary School, Fauldhouse

Spring And Summer

Spring
Cold, raining
Growing, flying, digging
Robin, leaves, birds, sun
Playing, swimming, planning
Hot, sunny
Summer.

Mia Coleman (9)

St John The Baptist RC Primary School, Fauldhouse

Sad And Happy

Sad
Emotional, unhappy
Hyper, crying, loud
Person, tear, video, friend
Dancing, sports, playing
Smile, smiley
Happy.

Marcel Wawrzak (9)

St John The Baptist RC Primary School, Fauldhouse

Spring And Autumn

Spring
Rainy, wet
Watery, digging, running
Warm, flowers, conkers, leaf
Falling, dying, stormy
Dry, wet
Autumn.

Campbell Young (9)

St John The Baptist RC Primary School, Fauldhouse

Cats

C ats eat cat food
A nd wander about themselves
T hey have cat toys
S o they don't get bored.

Kayla Paterson (6) & Declan

St John The Baptist RC Primary School, Fauldhouse

Dogs

D ogs eat dog food

O r dog treats and dog bones

G oing for a walk for exercise

S o they stay fit.

Rhegan O'Driscoll (6)

St John The Baptist RC Primary School, Fauldhouse

Dogs

D ogs eat dog food
O r dog treats and bones
G oing for walks for exercise
S o they can stay fit.

Leon Gillespie (5)
St John The Baptist RC Primary School, Fauldhouse

Cats

C ats can purr

A nd wander about themselves

T hey have cat toys

S o they don't get bored.

Lewis Macleod (6)

St John The Baptist RC Primary School, Fauldhouse

Cats

C ats eat cat food
A nd wander about
T hey have cat toys
S o they don't get bored.

Maisie Delaney (6)

St John The Baptist RC Primary School, Fauldhouse

Cats

C ats can jump
A nd run about
T hey will play with dogs
S o they don't get tired.

Safiyyah Sowe (6)
St John The Baptist RC Primary School, Fauldhouse

My Favourite Things

H ristiana is my name and my favourite thing in the whole world is my cute energetic dog

R uby-red is my least favourite colour but pink is my choice of colour

I ndulging in my mouth, melted beloved Dairy Milk chocolate is my dream

S ometimes when the sun is shining, I have a trip to the wonderful, beautiful beach

T owers are a little taller than my long luscious hair

I will always be there for my friends through thick and thin

A lso, every year it feels like it has been centuries

N oticing the navy clothes look at me as I enter the shops always makes my eyes bulge from my face

A nother thing about me, I have hazel coffee-coloured eyes and brown hair as long as Rapunzel's.

Hristiana Atlanasova (9)

St Mary's Catholic Primary School, Fleetwood

I Am Me

L ily is my name and I'm nine years old, I don't like pickled onions and I have a cute, fluffy dog

I nterestingly, the worst thing in the world are reptiles. They're slimy and scary and also yawn

L illie is my best friend, she's quite a fun, sporty kid. Summer is our favourite season and we're always on a whizz

Y ear by year, I've become smarter but then that big school will come and grab you and eat you up like a colossal dinosaur

M ysteriously I adore art, I splat and sketch colour and shade

A dditionally, I have two fish. I haven't called them anything but one of them is fat and the other is really skinny

R oses are good but lilies are perfect, they smell beautiful and they brighten up the pond

T owers is the short name for Alton Towers. So many ginormous rides that go whizz, boom, zoom!

I ncluding Blackpool Pleasure Beach, its the best place ever! The best things are the chips, the attractions, the roller coasters and much more!

N o, no, no! I'm not going on that scary walk. It's creepy and very scary!

Lily Martin (9)
St Mary's Catholic Primary School, Fleetwood

Kobey Kebab

K obey is my fab name and my favourite thing in the world is my amazing Xbox

O range is one of my favourite colours but blue is my favourite colour

B y the way, I am very fast; as fast as a cheetah I will have you know

E ngland, who are my home football team, are one of the best international teams of all time

Y early a game called FIFA comes out, I always manage to get it because I am lucky me

R arely I get a rest in school, however, I can have a rest whenever I want to at home

E very day, my mum and dad tell me to gel my hair - I never do it

E arly in the morning (7am) I rise from my den, energetically scoff my breakfast, brush my shiny white teeth and set off to school

C heating is something I never do and never will do no matter the situation

E nglish and maths are a piece of cake for me, it is geography I struggle with.

Kobey Reece (10)

St Mary's Catholic Primary School, Fleetwood

Molly's Poem

M y name is Molly, I'm autistic

O nly I understand this but English is a piece of cake, however, maths is a ticking time bomb!

L et me tell you this, school is a trillion seconds long

L iterally, I lost a friend when I was one

Y ou might not believe this but I was in intensive care for one night when I was a baby

M y favourite season is spring because life rises hastily

I love Christmas because it's like your happiness is about to overfill your head

L isten to this, wherever you go in school, noise dances to its deafening beat

H ow is your life?

E very day is a chance to restart like a ray of sunshine, hit the restart button

N ever mess with me because I'm a fierce, brave girl

C an you think of an acrostic poem?

H ell isn't me, I'm also kind and sensible.

Molly Milhench (9)

St Mary's Catholic Primary School, Fleetwood

Karolyn Is My Name

K arolyn is my name, I love animals like large, fat elephants and cute, fluffy dogs

A lso I like to swim like a dolphin gliding through the pool, never mind the temperature, it is always very cool

R iding my bike on the beach is beautiful, loyal and friendly are what people call me

O riginally from Bulgaria and England, I love my family (sister, Mum and Dad). They are courageous and loyal

L oving, caring, kind and trustworthy are some of my amazing over the moon personalities, as talented as Albert Einstein

Y ou're lucky if you meet me and my amazing personality, it will always be lovely

N avy and light blue are my favourite colours. My eyes are brown and dreamy chocolate. My smile is as soft as a teddy bear. My luscious, medium-length hair is the colour of hot chocolate. Once in a blue moon, I feel under the weather.

Karolyn Hristova (11)
St Mary's Catholic Primary School, Fleetwood

This Is Me - Fantastic Florence

F lorence is my name, you may know I share it with the first-ever fantastic nurse of the NHS

L ollipops sour as lemons melt in my mouth. They are my favourite sweets in the whole wide world. I could eat a million tasty treats

O ccasionally I visit my dad's house and we go to the park together as the birds sing their song

R eally cute are sloths, they are my most treasured toys, loving them is a piece of cake

E very day I attend my wonderful caring school - the days are busy, they fly by

N o one can stop me from loving sloths. They are so cute, soft and fluffy, they never stop being lazy

C ucumber is a daily snack, I adore them with all my heart

E veryone at school is my friend, especially the ones that make me happy.

Florence Martinez (10)

St Mary's Catholic Primary School, Fleetwood

My Life

R alica is my name and I have eight pets: my three cute fluffy hamsters, two lazy turtles, two poofy dogs and my spiky hedgehog - they are the most playful energetic pets in the world

A ll in all I love chocolate as much as I love my family (but obviously I love my family more)

L uckily when I am feeling down, sunny days make me smile like a glistening ball of fire

I ndulging in the melted chocolate which is velvety in my mouth. I always feel like I am in Heaven eating it

C ontributing to my important role of deputy head girl, meetings are important - they are vital

A nyways, I'm going to go now, hope you have an amazing day and always have a smile on your face and I hope your smile lights up any room!

Ralica Parapanova (10)

St Mary's Catholic Primary School, Fleetwood

All About Me!

R uby is my name and I am a 9-year-old girl. I enjoy a lot of things, especially sports

U K is where I live, it has loads of amazing sights

B lue is one of my favourite colours as well as purple and pastel-green (they are the best colours of the rainbow)

Y ou're lucky if you get to meet me and my amazing personality because it's hard to beat

L uckily, when I'm feeling down, sunny days make me smile especially when the glistening ball of fire smiles down on me

E asily I keep a lot of secrets and I never spill the tea - hyphens are important in my life

A s I have mentioned, I love art but as well as loving art I also love my family because they always make me smile.

Ruby-Lea Mynott Ward (9)

St Mary's Catholic Primary School, Fleetwood

Callum

C allum is my name and I like to play out with my brother, out on the tall green mount

A t my small, perfect house, I like to play on the Xbox. Fortnite is my favourite game, the graphics are spectacular

L et me get my costume on, my dream costume is a blue exoskeleton. Instead of spill the beans, I'm hoping people spill the candy into my mummy's basket

L ovely days are for when the sun smiles down, these days are for playing out in the fresh sea air

U nder the tree lies my Christmas present, my mountainous pile, as welcoming as a fifty-star restaurant

M ullac is my name spelt backwards. I think it's funny to look at things in a different way.

Callum Watson (10)
St Mary's Catholic Primary School, Fleetwood

Jessica

J essica is my name, I'm a funny and smart girl that enjoys cooking, art and make-up

E ating, drawing and shopping are things I enjoy, my favourite thing is my family

S ummer is my top-tier season and I like having fun in the sun

S miling is what I like doing, I don't like being upset or having bad days but when the sun smiles back at me it brightens my day

I have medium, crystal-blue eyes, creamy golden hair and I am tall for my age

C aring, kindness and honesty are some of my extraordinary features; I will never spill the beans

A zure-blue, lavender-purple and pastel colours (especially yellow) are my favourite colours.

Jessica Grimshaw (10)

St Mary's Catholic Primary School, Fleetwood

Lucy Rose

L ucky Lucy everyone calls me. Perhaps one day I will find a four-leaf clover!

U nlikely to see me, I have lots of energy and don't stay still for long so be amazed as I zoom past

C ollege is something I might do in the future, I grow my brain like Einstein

Y awning like a sloth at the end of the day, I love being tucked up in bed

R oses are red, violets are blue. I enjoy PE, how about you?

O nce in a while when the sun smiles down, I enjoy playing out with my friends

S ent to the market and to the shops, I never have a moment's peace in my house

E very day when I go to school, I take a bath.

Lucy Rose (10)
St Mary's Catholic Primary School, Fleetwood

Layla's Great

L ayla is my wonderful name and my favourite thing to ride is my bright beautiful bike

A wesome apples are my favourite but I like green, brown, freckly pears for my breakfast

Y esterday I asked my sister if I could have a blue and white Stitch birthday cake. I doubt I'll get one though. She only says yes once in a blue moon

L ater one day, after school, there was an old lady that needed help so I went up to her and said, "Do you need help?" She said, "Yes."

A nywhere I go, my hair swings and sways, it is like Rapunzel's hair which means it is hard to put up. It's a nightmare for me when I go swimming!

Layla Carney (10)

St Mary's Catholic Primary School, Fleetwood

Gracie Is Great

G racie is my name, my favourite thing in the whole world is my fluffy, cute dog Bridget the midget

R abbits are one of my friends, they hop around and are completely adorable

A dditionally, chocolate is all I want on a cold winter's day

C ollecting a dazzling array of breathtakingly sparkly gems is exciting, their jagged edges are as sharp as claws

I f I get told a secret, I will never spill the beans. I'm an honest friend. I will be a good friend

E arly in the morning I get up and can't wait to see the sun shining down on me. Eyes as green as grass. Like a leaf when winter comes and I slouch like a beast.

Gracie Penton (10)

St Mary's Catholic Primary School, Fleetwood

Mateusz

M y crystal-blue eyes shine in the sun and glitter for days

A ll of my dogs were the strongest dogs in the world

T housands of thoughts came to my mind when I got the ball at training, my mum broke my leg at the next match

E verybody tells me their secrets but I never spill the beans

U rgently my mum gave me a tenner and told me to keep the savings

S ince it was my birthday two days ago, I'm eleven going on 18

Z apping my hand because of the phone was a silly mistake. I don't think I will spend that long on it again.

Mateusz Krysztofinska (11)

St Mary's Catholic Primary School, Fleetwood

My Fantastic Name

D aisey is my name, I love to play games. I feel like my TV is showing what I am doing in real life

A fternoons are not that bad but the morning takes forever just to get to lunch

I feel like I'm melting in a river that will not stop until I fly high in the sky

S ometimes I feel like I'm melting into a million blobs. I'm as smooth as butter when I want to be

E xpressing my feelings like my heart is full of all the universe's happiness

Y ellow is beautiful - it reminds me of the sunflower painting by van Gogh.

Daisey Gawne (10)

St Mary's Catholic Primary School, Fleetwood

My Name Is Georgi

G eorgi is my name and I look after my adorable, energetic dog

E xtinct dinosaurs I find very interesting, their speed fascinates me

O nce I get older, I wish to be Michael Phelps at swimming

R iding my black, stylish scooter across the mount pack is what I enjoy doing, especially when the sun smiles down

G oing to Bulgaria is what I love the most, it never rains cats and dogs there - the sky is always blue

I n the future, I hope to be a gamer earning millions of fabulous followers.

Georgi Mitov (10)

St Mary's Catholic Primary School, Fleetwood

Blake Is My Name

B ees and wasps are my biggest fear because I have never been stung before, plus all my friends are scared so I jumped on the bandwagon

L ovely, beautiful lakes are what I like to gaze at all day

A ches are what pro-footballer have, like great swimmers

K nuckleball is a thing in football which is very rare

E ggs are what you use in a pancakes. When you crack them sometimes look like they are staring back at us

Blake Slinger (9)

St Mary's Catholic Primary School, Fleetwood

The Cat Man

C onner is my name and my most favourite thing in the whole world is my fat, cuddly cat called Amber

O n my list I see that I go swimming every Saturday

N ever have I ever liked squishy, slippery tomatoes

N o one would think my favourite colour is pink

E ven I know my favourite superhero is the heroic and exciting Spider-Man

R eading my book, I take a peek and look to see I have soft, silky hair.

Conner Watson (10)

St Mary's Catholic Primary School, Fleetwood

Elliot The Great

E lliot is my name and I am ten

L ight as a feather, that is my eldest sister

L acey is my sassy sister, she is younger

I n my mouth is delicious white chocolate

O cean-blue skies are beautiful

T he cute dogs are cute even the dogs with smiley eyes.

Elliot Wilson (10)

St Mary's Catholic Primary School, Fleetwood

Flash

F lash is so silly

L oves chasing the ball

A lways licking everyone

S itting on his bed

H e is a lunatic.

Finley Marshall (7)

Stanley St Andrew's CE Primary School, Stanley

Mischief And Tricks

I like fun that is funny
I like food that is yummy
I get into trouble when the weather is not sunny
The hat that sits on my head
Is stripy colours white and red
I like to rhyme words like this and that
Did you guess?
I'm the Cat in the Hat.

George Kebell (11)
Starcross Primary School, Starcross

Foxy The Last Fox

A fox named Foxy
R eally was
C old and lost
T hen she scuttled around
I t was getting dark
C oco the wolf came, she was a

F riend, she was lost too!
O h Foxy, are you okay? No, she wasn't
X i, my mum, there you are!
Y ou're lost too, Coco, come here and get
nice and warm!

Violet Wilson (7)
Strandtown Primary School, Belfast

Autumn

A pples above our heads
U nder the tree we see smashed berries
T ree branches swaying gently
U p above the leaves are
M any floating to the ground
N est-building all around.

Shaun Mathew (8)
Strandtown Primary School, Belfast

Nature

I can hear the sweet autumn rain
I can smell the damp, fresh dew
I can feel the heat of the fire
I can taste the hot marshmallow
I can see the little hedgehog scurrying around.

Lucie Wilson (7)
Strandtown Primary School, Belfast

Our World

S tars are bright in the sky
P lanets go around the sun
A stronauts are people who go into space
C onstellations sparkling
E arth is our planet.

Yuriy Hramov (7)

Strandtown Primary School, Belfast

Rusty

R ustling of the leaves
U nder the tree
S itting on crunchy leaves
T rying to find colourful leaves
Y ellow and orange and green.

Matthew Lucas (7)

Strandtown Primary School, Belfast

It's Raining Cats And Dogs

Dogs
Fluffy, cute
Barking, eating, walking
Toys, treats, posts, mice
Purring, scratching, pouncing
Smooth, soft
Cats.

Saul Farrell (8)

Strandtown Primary School, Belfast

The Seaside

I love to go to the seaside where the sea
crashes onto the sand
The ebbing and flowing of the tide and the
sand trickling through my hand
The fish and chips smell lovely, the
candyfloss smells sweet
The children are so bubbly, there is nothing
more unique
The seagulls linger all day eyeing up their
picnics, they will never go away until they
have their sandwiches fixed
The slimy seaweed and the spiky shells stay
on show in the rock pools
The children take their buckets and spades
to make sandcastles and wishing wells
That was the end of the day for them and
they wish to come back again.

Sian Keeling (9)
Windsor Park CE Middle School, Uttoxeter

Hogwarts

Down in the dark dungeons
Professor Snape is walking around checking
all the potions
Bubbling and boiling away in their dark,
dingy cauldrons
Lots of toad legs scattered around
And Snape yelling instructions to the
petrified First Years.

Meanwhile, if you wander furthermore
towards the Great Hall
You will see Sixth Years
Learning to apparate into hoops
Often splinting themselves in two.

In the Gryffindor common room
You will see stressed Seventh Years revising
for their NEWTs
Yelling at the other years
For making too much of a hullabaloo.

If you listen harder
You can hear all the owls calling loudly
Hoping to be picked.

Holly Chapman (10)
Windsor Park CE Middle School, Uttoxeter

The Fabulous Flamingo

One day the trees were full of mango
Where there lay a fabulous flamingo
Every day she would stare at a tree
Where a person would climb that tree
And the person's name was Bea
She felt sad because she wanted to be like her
Then she did a humongous jump into the river
She tried and tried, day after day, but she couldn't do it
Then one day she felt a particular feeling in her stomach
That she could do it finally
She took a leap with a peach
She finally did it and that is why she is a fabulous flamingo!

Thea Clarke (9)
Windsor Park CE Middle School, Uttoxeter

Looking After Our Birds In Winter

Looking after our birds in winter is an
important thing to do
While we are all warm and cosy inside we
need to think about the birds outside
I feed the robins and sparrows every day
I go out in the cold fresh air
The grass crunches under my feet as I go
All the birds chirp and tweet whilst I replace
the frozen water in their bath
Then I top up their seed
Standing and looking at my garden
There is snow on the tips of the pine needles
And all across the ground
I can feel my feet going numb.

Nancy Newton (9)
Windsor Park CE Middle School, Uttoxeter

Cheese

Cheese, cheese, cheese - my favourite thing to eat
It's made with milk and acid and a little bit of heat
From milky curd like cottage cheese that's soft and smells milky and creamy
To strong cheddar that you wouldn't eat with peas
That is hard and salty and definitely not stinky
Brie is really quite smelly, it smells like rotting feet
Stinky like it's been inside a welly
My favourite is halloumi, it comes with rosemary, mint or chilli
And on your teeth it is squeaky.

Joseph Clarke (9)
Windsor Park CE Middle School, Uttoxeter

Tomatoes

Some tomatoes are red
Some tomatoes are yellow
Put them in a pan and just let them be
mellow
Let the sweet juicy, round things cook for a
while
And soon you will see, they can be crispy
and juicy
But they are all just for me!

If you want to feel the same as me
Grow your own tomatoes and soon you'll
see
Some tomatoes are red
Some tomatoes are yellow
Eat them whole, chopped or cooked
And if you do you will soon be hooked!

Connor Wilkes (9)
Windsor Park CE Middle School, Uttoxeter

My House

In my house I can hear Mummy and Daddy
talking, the TV talking and the cat walking
I can taste the food on my plate
I can taste my drinks but not lemonade
which I hate
I can smell our food and my cat's food
I can also smell Mummy's candles, they are
good
I can feel the clothes on me and the doors
around me
I see everything, including the TV outside my
bedroom
Then when I fall asleep, I don't see anything.

Ellie-May Wilson (9)
Windsor Park CE Middle School, Uttoxeter

Wintertime

Winter has arrived
There's snow everywhere
The trees have no leaves
So they look bare
The birds are enjoying their rest
All tucked up in their nests
Snow falling on them
Just like a little trickle
But soon the temperature will rise
And the rain appears
The snow slowly fades away
And spring rolls in
Many hours of play
Will fill our day!

William Chandler (9)
Windsor Park CE Middle School, Uttoxeter

Dogs

I hear the sound of the dogs barking to
each other in their back gardens
My hand becomes submerged as I touch his
soft, fluffy fur
That's disgusting
That smell of stinky dog breath
Left, right, left, right
Wagging tails in my sight
Yum-yum
What a tasty biscuit
Oh actually, that is not mine
It's the dog's - gross!
I do really love my dogs!

Lewis Frost (9)

Windsor Park CE Middle School, Uttoxeter

Friend

You're my friend and I hope you know that's
always going to be true
No matter what life throws at us, I will stand
right by you
In times of grief, I will give you belief
When you're upset, I'll be your shoulder
I'll be there whenever you need me to lend a
hand
To do a good deed
I will always be there for you right to the
end.

Maisie Rowntree (9)
Windsor Park CE Middle School, Uttoxeter

Holiday

I can see the beach, sandcastles and rock
pool
I can hear the waves coming in and out and
the children laughing and jumping about
I can feel the sand between my toes
I can smell the suncream on my nose
I can taste the mint choc chip ice cream in
my cone
Take me back to my holiday, I never want to
go home.

Henry Coates (10)
Windsor Park CE Middle School, Uttoxeter

The Dark Side

I can hear wings flying into the Imperial
I can see Stormtroopers firing their E-11
blaster rifles at me
I can taste the Naboo fruit, sweet on my
tongue, I am ready
I can feel the hot, red lightsaber in my hand
I can smell the smoke from the fire like an
invisible snake coiling itself around me.

Corey Lampitt (9)

Windsor Park CE Middle School, Uttoxeter

Christmas Day

I can hear the bells ringing from the church far away
I can see the snow on the ground, it is a beautiful Christmas Day
I can smell the turkey roasting on the baking tray
The oven is too hot to touch
My taste buds come alive with the food I love so much.

Benjamin Haywood (9)
Windsor Park CE Middle School, Uttoxeter

Maggie My Dog

M uddy wet paws

A cute wagging tail

G ot very sharp claws

G ets excited to steal the mail

I can hear her barks and pants from her jaws

E ver so fast, not like a snail.

Emilia Skinner (9)

Windsor Park CE Middle School, Uttoxeter

YoungWriters®
— Est. 1991 —

YOUNG WRITERS INFORMATION

We hope you have enjoyed reading this book – and that you will continue to in the coming years.

If you're the parent or family member of an enthusiastic poet or story writer, do visit our website **www.youngwriters.co.uk/subscribe** and sign up to receive news, competitions, writing challenges and tips, activities and much, much more! There's lots to keep budding writers motivated!

If you would like to order further copies of this book, or any of our other titles, then please give us a call or order via your online account.

Young Writers
Remus House
Coltsfoot Drive
Peterborough
PE2 9BF
(01733) 890066
info@youngwriters.co.uk

Join in the conversation!
Tips, news, giveaways and much more!

f YoungWritersUK **𝕏** YoungWritersCW **⊙** youngwriterscw